Occupational Standards

for Early Childhood Educators

**Child Care
Human Resources
Sector Council**

Occupational Standards for Early Childhood Educators.
ISBN 978-0-9781116-2-5

Issued also in French under the title: Normes professionnelles des éducatrices et éducateurs à l'enfance. ISBN 978-0-9781116-2-5

To request copies of this document or information contact:

Child Care Human Resources Sector Council
Suite 714, 151 Slater Street
Ottawa, Ontario, Canada. K1P 5H3
info@ccsc-cssge.ca
1-866-411-6960
www.ccsc-cssge.ca

Consultants: Future Learning Inc.
Editor: Ascribe Marketing Communications Inc.
Translation: Sylvie Payeur
Layout: Kim Nelson Design
Original Layout Design: Hangar 13 Art & Design
Cover Design: Richard Proulx

This project is funded by the Government
of Canada's Sector Council Program.

Canada

The opinions and interpretations in this publication are those of the author and do not necessarily reflect those of the Government of Canada.

CONTENTS
OCCUPATIONAL STANDARDS

THE CHILD CARE
HUMAN RESOURCES SECTOR COUNCIL

The Child Care Human Resources Sector Council (CCHRSC) is a pan-Canadian organization dedicated to moving forward on human resources (HR) issues in the child care sector. The CCHRSC brings together national partners and other sector representatives to help develop a confident, knowledgeable, skilled and respected workforce valued for its contribution to early childhood education and care.

A) Goals

The goals of the CCHRSC are to:

- Build and share knowledge to advance HR and labour market issues;
- Create tools to promote good HR management practices;
- Foster the development of a skilled workforce;
- Provide leadership and coordination on HR issues; and
- Engage sector stakeholders to ensure a comprehensive, coordinated and responsive approach.

B) Definition

The term 'child care' has often been used to describe the sector in which early childhood educators work. There has been much discussion over the past few years about what the name of the sector, as well as the titles for occupations within the sector, should be. It is understood that the discipline or knowledge base is early childhood education and care. Therefore, for the purposes of this document, the term 'early childhood educator' (ECE) will be used to define a person who provides education and care.

GUIDE TO THE
OCCUPATIONAL STANDARDS

INTRODUCTION

Introduction to occupational standards

A) What are occupational standards?

Occupational standards describe what a person in a particular occupation must know and be able to do to be considered 'capable' in the occupation—that is, the level of skills and knowledge required to do their job effectively, safely and properly.

These occupational standards are intended for ECEs working in an early childhood education and care environment. They apply to any ECE who provides education and care in programs for children aged 0-12 in a variety of age groupings, including infant and toddler care, preschool-aged care, school-aged care and inclusive care, in any of the following:

- Publicly funded child care settings
- Privately operated child care settings
- Home-based child care settings
- Family resource programs
- Other early childhood settings (e.g., nursery schools, kindergartens)

B) Why have occupational standards?

The development of occupational standards by the people doing the job enables them to take ownership of their occupation. They, rather than outsiders, define acceptable professional behaviour and the knowledge, skills and abilities required for competent practice.

Occupational standards also serve a wide range of other purposes within the child care sector, including:

For early childhood educators

- Offering a foundation for career development
- Identifying training gaps in the required occupational skill set
- Enhancing occupational recognition
- Enhancing job mobility

For employers

- Identifying key tasks and roles
- Identifying professional development needs
- Facilitating objective job descriptions
- Providing guidance for recruitment

For early childhood education faculty

- Identifying areas where expertise is required
- Providing the basis for curriculum, training development and education

For sector organizations

- Forming the basis of certification programs
- Forming the basis of program accreditation
- Creating professional development opportunities

For the stakeholders

- Identifying the skills required for specific occupations
- Providing nationally–recognized, sector-driven benchmarks of best practices
- Providing career development information for practitioners laddering to administration

C) What do occupational standards consist of?

To facilitate understanding of the nature of the occupation, the occupational standards document is presented as follows:

Section

The largest division within the analysis, each section reflects a distinct operation relevant to the occupation.

Task

A task is defined as a distinct, observable and measurable activity. When specific tasks are combined, they make up the logical and necessary steps required to complete a specific assignment within a section.

Context Statement

Defines the parameters of the task.

Sub-Task

The smallest practical division of any work activity. When specific sub-tasks are combined, they fully describe all duties constituting a task.

Required skills and abilities

The elements of skill and abilities an individual must acquire to adequately perform a sub-task. Skills and abilities may be acquired through formal education, on-the-job learning, self-study or experience.

Required core knowledge

The core knowledge an individual must acquire to adequately perform a sub-task. Knowledge may be acquired through formal education, on-the-job learning, self-study, experience or professional development.

D) To whom do these occupational standards apply?

These standards cover the broad range of tasks that can be performed by ECEs.

However, the occupational standards are not meant to replace individual job descriptions; they are to be used for guidance in defining skill levels and knowledge for ECEs in specific settings or positions. Early childhood educators may perform tasks in a number of key areas of the occupational standards, but not necessarily in all areas. For example, in large operations other individuals may be employed or designated to perform specific tasks.

DEVELOPMENT
OF THE OCCUPATIONAL STANDARDS

More than 900 ECEs with extensive knowledge and experience in early childhood education developed and validated these occupational standards through interviews, online surveys, regional workshops and provincial/territorial validation exercises.

It is important to note the following standards are a revision of the *Occupational Standards for Child Care Practitioners* developed by the Canadian Child Care Federation in 2003. This revision was completed to ensure that the occupational standards for ECEs were as reflective of the current roles and responsibilities as possible.

The occupational standards development process began early in 2009 with a literature review of existing provincial and international standards to determine the scope of the occupation and the approach to analyzing the occupation. Key informant interviews were conducted with leaders in early childhood education from across the country to identify occupational trends, qualifications and education, and issues affecting the early childhood educator. This information was used to gain insight from ECEs themselves regarding trends and changes in the profession, including how well graduates are prepared for working in the occupation. A total of 748 online surveys were completed by ECEs across the country. The survey responses aided in the definition of the scope for the occupational analysis and served to engage a wide cross-section of ECEs.

Each of these steps in the development process served to clarify that all distinct sectors of early childhood education—infant care, school-aged care, family child care, special needs and inclusion, and early childhood care in kindergarten settings—are essential to include in the definition of early childhood educator.

Using this broad definition, three occupational analysis workshops were held in Edmonton, Toronto and Montreal, during which the 43 participants developed the pan-Canadian occupational standards. The development of the occupational standards was followed by 12 validation workshops conducted in English and French with more than 150 participants from all provinces and territories.

SCOPE OF THE
EARLY CHILDHOOD EDUCATOR

An ECE is an individual who is responsible for the development, delivery and evaluation of the care and education of children ages 0-12 years in a variety of age groupings, including infant and toddler care, preschool-aged care, school-aged care and inclusive care. Early childhood educators may work in a variety of settings, including publicly-funded child care settings, privately-operated child care settings, home-based child care settings and family resource programs. The administrative/ business skills required for home-based child care are not included in these standards; these are covered in the Occupational Standards for Child Care Administrators (CCHRSC 2006).

In smaller operations, particularly home-based child care, ECEs function as educator, caregiver and administrator. Some ECEs work with a variety of age groups, while others specialize in a particular age or group setting. As the early childhood environment changes, more and more child care settings are requiring educators with higher or more specialized skills to work with children with special and multiple needs.

The role of the ECE includes the planning and delivery of inclusive play-based learning and care programs for children in order to promote the well-being and holistic development of children. This includes the delivery of programs from infancy to preschool children and school-aged children, including children with special needs, ECEs are also responsible for the assessment of the programs and of the progress of children in the programs, as well as communicating with the parents or persons with legal custody of the children in the programs in order to improve the development of the children.

Regardless of the setting, ECEs facilitate daily experiences that support and promote each child's physical, language, emotional, cognitive and creative development and behaviour while respecting inclusion principles and the diversity of the population.

In the delivery of programming, ECEs complete a variety of health and safety procedures and comply with quality standards, current laws and regulations associated with a healthy and safe environment. They follow health and safety practices to develop and maintain a safe environment for children by performing regular equipment and facilities inspections.

As a part of holistic approach, ECEs form collaborative partnerships with children's families that honour the family's role as primary caregiver and respect each family's composition, language and culture. They also establish relationships with and use the resources of the children's communities to support the achievement of program objectives.

Early childhood educators advocate for support from governmental agencies and associations for children and their families by communicating clear, accurate information. They work as members of teams to develop learning environments that support productive work and meet professional needs, recognize and capitalize on the strengths of fellow team members and provide mutual support, collaboration and assistance.

Early childhood educators demonstrate professionalism by participating in ongoing professional development and learning, by following a Code of Ethics, maintaining required certifications and registrations, and respecting the rights of children and their families by maintaining confidentiality while maintaining appropriate records and documentation.

ANALYSIS

SECTION A
CHILD DEVELOPMENT, LEARNING AND CARE

Task A.1	Facilitate the development and behaviour of children.

Context Statement:

Early Childhood Educators facilitate daily experiences that support and promote each child's physical, language, emotional, cognitive, social and creative development and behaviour using applicable observation tools while respecting inclusion principles and diversity issues.

Sub-Task A.1.1

USE A VARIETY OF OBSERVATION AND DOCUMENTATION TECHNIQUES.

Required skills and abilities	Required core knowledge
ECEs are able to:	*ECEs know:*
a) document observations using a range of methods (e.g., notes, photos, videos);	1) child development theories;
b) seek information from parents' observations of their children;	2) effective communication skills to understand and interpret children's behaviours;
c) categorize observations into development domains;	3) theories and approaches about observation and documentation techniques.
d) interpret observations;	
e) communicate observations with team and families;	
f) use non-biased language (e.g., open-ended sentences, non-judgemental terminology).	

Sub-Task A.1.2

FACILITATE COGNITIVE DEVELOPMENT OF CHILDREN.

Required skills and abilities	Required core knowledge
ECEs are able to:	*ECEs know:*
a) assess and interpret developmental stage of children;	1) cognitive development related to age of the children;
b) observe the children's play and interactions;	2) multiple intelligences;
c) interpret observations;	3) program and quality standards regarding observation techniques and cognitive development;
d) identify strategies to further promote cognitive development;	4) communication skills to obtain information about the child;
e) gather information about the child's cognitive development from team members, family and relevant others.	5) resources in the environment (e.g., colleagues, materials, students).

Sub-Task A.1.3

FACILITATE LANGUAGE DEVELOPMENT OF CHILDREN.

Required skills and abilities	Required core knowledge
ECEs are able to:	*ECEs know:*
a) observe and interpret language development during play and interactions;	1) language development for second language learners;
b) communicate with the child (e.g., non-verbal techniques, home language(s));	2) child development theories;
c) determine language(s) spoken in the home;	3) language development theories according to developmental stages and ages;
d) determine language ability according to age and stage of development;	4) developmental practices for promoting and supporting language development;
e) identify factors affecting language capacity (e.g., environmental, intellectual, cultural, physiological);	5) resources in the environment (e.g., colleagues, materials, students);
f) identify beliefs and practices that affect language use and development.	6) multiple intelligences;
	7) program and quality standards regarding observation techniques and language development;
	8) cultural diversity theories and approaches.

Sub-Task A.1.4

FACILITATE SOCIAL DEVELOPMENT OF CHILDREN.

Required skills and abilities	Required core knowledge

ECEs are able to:
 	
a) observe:
 	
   • the child's interaction with peers and adults;
 	
   • the child when they are being dropped off and picked up;
 	
   • the child's stage of social play;
 	
   • the child's interaction with their environment;
 	
   • the child's body language, gestures and facial expressions;
 	
   • the child's peer entry group skills;
 	
   • how the child manages stress and conflicts;
 	
   • how the child manages transition times in the program;
 	
b) identify triggers that may impact on the child's social behaviour (e.g., transitions);
 	
c) facilitate children's problem-solving skills;
 	
d) facilitate children's entry skills.
	ECEs know:
	
	1) child development theories;
	
	2) child social development theories;
	
	3) multiple intelligences;
	
	4) diversity theories and approaches;
	
	5) program and quality standards regarding observation techniques and social development;
	
	6) the child's family and extended network of support;
	
	7) resources in the environment (e.g., colleagues, materials, students).

Sub-Task A.1.5

FACILITATE ACCEPTANCE OF DIVERSITY.

Required skills and abilities	Required core knowledge
ECEs are able to:	*ECEs know:*
a) model a positive attitude towards diversity (e.g., family, cultural, special needs);	1) differing socioeconomic and cultural realities within the program;
b) provide materials and activities that reflect diversity;	2) immigrant adjustment process;
c) check and validate perceptions (e.g., why a child does not look an adult in the eye);	3) concepts of discrimination, prejudice, homophobia, racism, etc.
d) promote positive attitudes towards differences;	
e) utilize different communication methods.	

Sub-Task A.1.6

FACILITATE EMOTIONAL DEVELOPMENT OF CHILDREN.

Required skills and abilities	Required core knowledge
ECEs are able to:	*ECEs know:*
a) observe:	1) child development theories;
• the child's interactions at drop-off and pick-up;	2) child temperament theories;
• the child's interactions with family members;	3) attachment theories;
• the child during play with other children and adults;	4) multiple intelligences;
b) assess and interpret:	5) self-regulation skills development theories;
• how the child relates to others;	6) program and quality standards regarding observation techniques and emotional development;
• the child's self-esteem and autonomy, self-concept and self-identity;	7) planning processes and theories;
• the child's level of comfort or security;	8) resources in the environment (e.g., colleagues, materials, students).
• the child's problem-solving strategies;	
• how the child manages stress and conflict;	
• how transition times affect the child;	
• how the child plays within their environment;	
• if the child displays developmentally appropriate empathy;	
• the child's self-regulation skills;	
c) implement strategies:	
• set goals;	
• review;	
• evaluate and reflect.	

Sub-Task A.1.7

FACILITATE CREATIVE DEVELOPMENT OF CHILDREN.

Required skills and abilities	Required core knowledge
ECEs are able to:	*ECEs know:*
a) facilitate children in the planning and follow-through of activities;	1) resources in the environment (e.g., colleagues, materials, students);
b) structure the environment and activities around creative learning;	2) active learning principles (e.g., key experiences);
c) provide open-ended activities with varied stimulating materials;	3) multiple intelligences;
d) facilitate children's problem-solving skills;	4) multiple teaching strategies;
e) set up the environment to promote creative development;	5) program and quality standards regarding observation techniques and creative development.
f) provide activities that enable the children to express their creativity;	
g) demonstrate creativity, spontaneity and flexibility.	

Sub-Task A.1.8

FACILITATE PHYSICAL DEVELOPMENT OF CHILDREN.

Required skills and abilities	Required core knowledge

ECEs are able to:
 	
a) observe and interpret:
   • the child's gross motor skills;
   • the child's fine motor skills;
   • how the child interacts with peers;
b) identify if the child may have physical challenges or disabilities;
c) identify individual circumstances that could affect physical development (e.g., premature birth);
d) implement strategies:
   • set goals;
   • review;
   • evaluate and reflect.
	ECEs know:
	
	1) child development theories;
	2) multiple intelligences;
	3) each child and their individual circumstances;
	4) program and quality standards regarding observation techniques and physical development;
	5) resources in the environment (e.g., colleagues, materials, students).

Task A.2 — Develop, implement and evaluate programs.

Context Statement:

In partnership with families, Early Childhood Educators research information to develop and implement programs that meet the developmental needs of the children within their settings, as determined by the age groups and stages of development of children with which they work. Through the use of a variety of observation methods and techniques, ECEs note the progress of each child within the various domains of child development.

Sub-Task A.2.1

RESEARCH A VARIETY OF CURRICULUM MODELS.

Required skills and abilities	Required core knowledge
ECEs are able to: a) research appropriate information about a range of curriculum approaches and models; b) analyze information from each model to determine the best fit with individual program needs.	*ECEs know:* 1) child development theories; 2) curriculum theories; 3) diversity of family contexts; 4) professional research tools and approaches (e.g., books, publications, reputable Internet sites); 5) philosophy of the program; 6) requirements of the program.

Sub-Task A.2.2
IMPLEMENT INCLUSION POLICY.

Required skills and abilities	Required core knowledge
ECEs are able to:	*ECEs know:*
a) develop inclusionary practices for program delivery;	1) inclusion policies and procedures;
b) implement inclusionary practices into programs;	2) principles of universal design and how they support inclusion of all children;
c) implement an inclusive environment for children;	3) different aspects of inclusion (e.g., cultural, general, sexual orientation, special needs);
d) promote inclusion within the program.	4) variety of diverse family compositions.

Sub-Task A.2.3

DEVELOP INFANT PROGRAM.

Required skills and abilities	Required core knowledge
ECEs are able to:	*ECEs know:*
a) develop a program based on: • observations; • developmental needs of children; • interests of children; • community resources; b) set up a physical environment that supports the child's learning and development; c) find resources and materials based on the child's interests and needs; d) set up a safe physical environment for activities; e) develop a written plan that includes activities; f) collaborate with parents in developing individual infant program plans; g) respect and respond to parents' expectations for their child; h) create an emotional bond with the child based on social and emotional needs; i) post the plan and review ongoing progress; j) exchange information and share observations daily on the infant's experience (e.g., eating, sleeping, milestones, play).	1) child development theories; 2) individual children and their families; 3) variety of diverse family compositions; 4) developmentally-enriched activities to develop skills; 5) attachment theories; 6) temperament theories; 7) related regulations, standards of practice, quality standards and licensing requirements; 8) organizational values, policies and procedures; 9) development of infant programs; 10) principles of establishing a developmentally-appropriate environment.

Sub-Task A.2.4

DEVELOP TODDLER PROGRAM.

Required skills and abilities	Required core knowledge
ECEs are able to:	*ECEs know:*
a) develop a program based on:	1) child development theories;
• observations;	2) individual children and their families;
• developmental needs of children;	3) related regulations, standards of practice, quality standards and licensing requirements;
• interests of children;	4) organizational values, policies and procedures.
• community resources;	
b) set up a physical environment that supports the child's learning and development;	
c) find resources and materials based on the child's interests and needs;	
d) respect and respond to parents' expectations for their child;	
e) follow continuum of development to enrich skills and abilities;	
f) offer a variety of activities and allow for revisiting;	
g) create an emotional bond with the child based on social and emotional needs;	
h) document and share program plan or make learning visible through a variety of means;	
i) involve parents in developing program plan;	
j) set up a safe physical environment for activities;	
k) provide parents with updates on their child's progress and development;	
l) support each child's full participation.	

Sub-Task A.2.5

DEVELOP PRE-SCHOOL PROGRAM.

Required skills and abilities	Required core knowledge
ECEs are able to:	*ECEs know:*
a) develop a program based on: • observations; • developmental needs of children; • interests of children; • community resources;	1) child development theories; 2) individual children and their families; 3) related regulations, standards of practice, quality standards and licensing requirements;
b) set up a physical environment that supports the child's learning and development;	4) organizational values, policies and procedures;
c) find resources and materials based on the child's interests and needs;	5) provincial/territorial early learning curriculum framework or program standard, as it applies;
d) follow continuum of development to enrich skills and abilities;	6) principles of equity to support of each child's full participation;
e) offer a variety of activities and allow for revisiting;	7) strategies to engage each child's unique strengths into the program.
f) create an emotional bond with the child based on social and emotional needs;	
g) document and share program plan or make learning visible through a variety of means;	
h) take parents' suggestions into consideration;	
i) respect and respond to parents' expectations for their child;	
j) set up a safe physical environment for activities;	
k) organize field trips based on philosophy of the program;	
l) promote environmentally-friendly activities (e.g., recycling, composting);	
m) facilitate the transition of children from child care to the school system;	
n) provide parents with updates on their child's progress and development.	

Sub-Task A.2.6

DEVELOP KINDERGARTEN-AGE PROGRAM.

Required skills and abilities	Required core knowledge
ECEs are able to:	*ECEs know:*
a) develop a program based on:	1) child development theories;
• observations;	2) individual children and their families;
• developmental needs of children;	3) related regulations, standards of practice, quality standards and licensing requirements;
• interests of children;	4) organizational values, policies and procedures;
• community resources;	5) policies and procedures of school, school board and Ministry/Department of Education;
• length and type of program (e.g., full days, alternative days, half days);	6) principles of equity to support of each child's full participation;
b) set up a physical environment that supports the child's learning and development;	7) kindergarten framework/curriculum.
c) find resources and materials based on the child's interests and needs;	
d) follow continuum of development to enrich skills and abilities;	
e) offer a variety of activities and allow for revisiting;	
f) create an emotional bond with the child based on social and emotional needs;	
g) document and post program plan;	
h) take parents' suggestions into consideration;	
i) respect and respond to parents' expectations for their child;	
j) incorporate child's goals;	
k) set up a safe physical environment for activities;	
l) organize field trips based on philosophy of the program;	
m) promote environmentally-friendly activities (e.g., recycling, composting);	
n) develop communication strategies between the school and the centre, if applicable;	
o) provide parents with updates on their child's progress and development.	

Sub-Task A.2.7

DEVELOP SCHOOL-AGE PROGRAM.

Required skills and abilities	Required core knowledge
ECEs are able to:	*ECEs know:*
a) engage children in the development of plans;	1) child development theories;
b) develop a program based on:	2) individual children and their families;
• observations;	3) related regulations, standards of practice, quality standards and licensing requirements;
• developmental needs of children;	
• interests of children;	4) organizational values, policies and procedures;
• community resources;	
• length and type of program (e.g., before and after school, full days, professional development days);	5) policies and procedures of school, school board and Ministry/Department of Education;
c) implement programs that are free of racism, sexism and homophobia;	6) principles of equity to support of each child's full participation.
d) encourage awareness of social justice issues to support the child's moral development;	
e) set up a physical environment that supports the child's learning and development;	
f) find resources and materials based on the child's interests and needs;	
g) follow continuum of development to enrich skills and abilities;	
h) offer a variety of activities and allow for revisiting;	
i) create an emotional bond with the child based on social and emotional needs;	
j) respect children's transition to adolescence;	
k) document and share program plan or make learning visible through a variety of means;	
l) take parents' suggestions into consideration;	
m) respect and respond to parents' expectations for their child;	
n) incorporate the child's goals;	
o) set up a safe physical environment for activities;	
p) organize field trips based on philosophy of the program;	
q) promote environmentally-friendly activities (e.g., recycling, composting);	
r) communicate and collaborate with other partners (e.g., schools, other professionals);	
s) provide parents with updates on their child's progress and development.	

Sub-Task A.2.8

DEVELOP MULTI-AGE PROGRAM.

Required skills and abilities	Required core knowledge
ECEs are able to:	*ECEs know:*
a) develop a program based on: • observations; • broad range of developmental needs of children; • interests of children; • community resources; b) set up a physical environment that supports the child's learning and development; c) find resources and materials based on the child's interests and needs; d) set up and maintain environment according to the skills and abilities of the children across the age range, taking safety aspects into consideration; e) program according to ages and developmental levels within the multi-age room; f) create an emotional bond with the children based on social and emotional needs; g) maintain ratios for multi-age groups; h) consider input from parents; i) respect and respond to parents' expectations for their children; j) promote environmentally-friendly activities (e.g., recycling, composting); k) provide parents with updates on their child's progress and development.	1) child development theories; 2) individual children and their families; 3) related regulations, standards of practice, quality standards and licensing requirements; 4) organizational values, policies and procedures; 5) strategies to engage each child's unique strengths into the program; 6) principles of equity to support of each child's full participation.

Sub-Task A.2.9

MODIFY ENVIRONMENT TO PROVIDE ACCESSIBILITY.

Required skills and abilities	Required core knowledge
ECEs are able to:	*ECEs know:*
a) provide accessibility for children and their parents;	1) specific needs of the children and their families;
b) adapt the environment to suit the specific needs of the child and the group;	2) inclusion policy of the program;
c) collaborate with colleagues and administration to prepare and maintain the setting;	3) core principles of reflective evaluation.
d) engage in ongoing reflective evaluation.	

Sub-Task A.2.10

IMPLEMENT PROGRAM.

Required skills and abilities	Required core knowledge
ECEs are able to:	*ECEs know:*
a) prepare the materials and environment;	1) child development theories;
b) introduce activities to the children;	2) related regulations, standards of practice, quality standards and licensing requirements;
c) promote activities to address the needs of all children (e.g., plan for diversity);	3) organizational values, policies and procedures;
d) respect and respond to parents' expectations for their children	4) program evaluation methods (e.g., best practices, quality standards);
e) vary play, routine and transitional periods (e.g., free play, directed play, projects, outdoors);	5) definition of learning, learning process and strategies to support learning;
f) use a variety of teaching/instruction strategies to support learning during play and small-group activities such as:	6) principles of equity to support of each child's full participation;
• observing;	7) evaluation analysis methods and strategies for program improvement and enrichment;
• asking open-ended questions;	8) reflective practice.
• giving children time to answer;	
• encouraging children to take turns;	
• providing positive encouragement, coaching and guidance;	
• demonstrating;	
• modelling;	
• scaffolding;	
• demonstrating flexibility;	
• transitioning between activities;	
g) explain rules and guidelines;	
h) ensure sufficient supplies;	
i) follow daily routines;	
j) adapt schedule when required.	

Sub-Task A.2.11

EVALUATE PROGRAM.

Required skills and abilities	Required core knowledge
ECEs are able to:	*ECEs know:*
a) observe and interpret:	1) child development theories;
• children's engagement in activities;	2) developmentally-enriching activities;
• children's ability to remain attentive;	3) safety guidelines, policies and practices;
b) actively interact with the children in a positive manner;	4) program evaluation methods;
c) identify if activity meets each child's:	5) evaluation analysis methods and strategies for program improvement and enrichment.
• physical development;	
• emotional development;	
• moral development;	
• social development;	
• language development;	
• cognitive development;	
• sexual development and gender identity;	
d) engage in reflective practice;	
e) seek and integrate feedback from parents;	
f) seek and integrate opinions from team;	
g) seek and integrate feedback from children;	
h) check that program meets guidelines and quality standards;	
i) draw relevant conclusions in written observations and discussions;	
j) make connections between observed behaviour and written observations and discussions;	
k) adjust program plan based on observations;	
l) prepare documentation (e.g., learning stories, language samples, children's drawings, emergent writing);	
m) provide parents with updates on their child's progress and development.	

Task A.3

Support the holistic development of all children.

Context Statement:

Early Childhood Educators recognize, promote and support the overall learning and development of children. They work to create trusting bonds and relationships with the children and create learning and development portfolios to document the development of each child.

Sub-Task A.3.1

BUILD MEANINGFUL RELATIONSHIPS WITH THE CHILDREN.

Required skills and abilities	Required core knowledge
ECEs are able to:	*ECEs know:*
a) empathize with the children;	1) child development theories;
b) engage in active listening;	2) attachment theories;
c) engage in respectful communication (e.g., positive language, tone of voice, position self at child's level, body language);	3) individual children's relationships with parents;
d) provide opportunities for children to experience success;	4) effective communication skills;
e) respond to the child's cues (e.g., verbal and non-verbal);	5) diverse approaches.
f) encourage the children (e.g., choices, problem solving, decision making);	
g) provide reassurance and support;	
h) demonstrate consistency in behaviour and consequences;	
i) develop a trusting bond with the child (e.g., teach respect of self, promote attachment, feeling of security, self-awareness and feeling of belonging).	

Sub-Task A.3.2

IDENTIFY AND EXPAND UPON LEARNING OPPORTUNITIES/TEACHABLE MOMENTS.

Required skills and abilities	Required core knowledge
ECEs are able to:	*ECEs know:*
a) observe children and interpret observations to plan curriculum;	1) child development theories;
b) identify and respond to learning opportunities/ teachable moments;	2) philosophy of the program;
c) demonstrate flexibility and spontaneity to take advantage of learning opportunities/teachable moments;	3) learning theories.
d) engage in active listening with the children;	
e) observe and respond to children's' feelings, interests and abilities;	
f) enter play to stimulate children's thinking and elaborate learning;	
g) choose/provide materials with properties that are related to the child's explorations in the indoor and outdoor environment;	
h) choose/provide materials with properties that are inclusive of all children and families in the group;	
i) plan activities that incorporate sensory and motor areas, physical knowledge skills and cognitive and social play levels;	
j) use a variety of resources available within the program;	
k) sustain play by providing opportunities for repeated practice;	
l) foster child-initiated activities.	

Sub-Task A.3.3

IDENTIFY AND SUPPORT THE CHILD'S INDIVIDUAL LEARNING AND DEVELOPMENT.

Required skills and abilities	Required core knowledge
ECEs are able to:	*ECEs know:*
a) observe children and interpret observations;	1) child development theories;
b) document the child's learning and development;	2) individual learning styles;
c) describe the child's representation (how the child demonstrates what he/she knows or explores);	3) available community and professional resources.
d) identify individual goals and objectives based on results of developmental observations;	
e) identify individual needs of the child;	
f) share observations with parents;	
g) engage in reflective practice;	
h) understand exceptionalities, special needs and differing abilities;	
i) develop individual programs and activities based on learning needs and styles of each child;	
j) develop activities within the program plan to help the child meet their goals and objectives;	
k) assess, interpret and record progress toward developmental goals and objectives;	
l) evaluate plan and make revisions if necessary;	
m) recommend to families the community agencies and resources available.	

Sub-Task A.3.4

IDENTIFY AND SUPPORT DIVERSITY, EQUITY AND INCLUSION.

Required skills and abilities	Required core knowledge
ECEs are able to:	*ECEs know:*
a) gather information about different forms of diversities (e.g., from the community, professional publications, websites);	1) specific cultures and diversities of children within the program and community;
b) meet with children and families to gather important information;	2) recognize diversity in race, sexual orientation, income and language;
c) accommodate different practices within the program;	3) professional sources (e.g., books, publications, community groups) on culture and diversity, equity and inclusion;
d) respect differences in families' parenting practices;	4) their own beliefs and how they affect their work/ self-awareness.
e) provide materials that are culturally inclusive, diverse and reflect an anti-bias approach;	
f) provide programs that reflect a diverse population;	
g) be sensitive and accepting of all children and their cultural, socioeconomic and family differences;	
h) engage all children in the program;	
i) promote and model the celebration of differences;	
j) provide opportunity for all children to learn about other cultures.	

Sub-Task A.3.5

MAINTAIN DOCUMENTATION OF THE CHILD'S DEVELOPMENT.

Required skills and abilities	Required core knowledge
ECEs are able to:	*ECEs know:*
a) document program planning;	1) curriculum theories;
b) develop a file for each child, including examples of the child's activities (e.g., photos, videos);	2) child development theories;
c) record daily observations of the children;	3) various observation methods and tools;
d) record behavioural and developmental progress;	4) documentation methods and tools.
e) provide parents with updates on their child's progress and development.	

Task A.4

Meet health, safety and well-being needs.

Context Statement:

Early Childhood Educators develop and maintain settings and environments that promote the health, welfare and safety of all children. They complete a variety of health and safety procedures and comply with quality standards, current laws and regulations associated with healthy and safe environments.

Sub-Task A.4.1

ACCOMMODATE FOR CHILDREN'S ALLERGIES.

Required skills and abilities	Required core knowledge
ECEs are able to:	*ECEs know:*
a) gather and post allergy information from families;	1) signs and symptoms of allergic reactions for individual children;
b) share observations with families;	2) when emergency care is required and how to administer care;
c) collaboratively develop an allergy response plan with parents for each applicable child;	3) federal/provincial/territorial/municipal regulations and quality standards;
d) follow the program's allergy policies;	4) program policies for administration of medication;
e) seek or administer treatment and first aid when required (e.g., administer EpiPen in the event of anaphylactic reactions);	5) risks of cross-contamination.
f) report and document allergic reactions.	

Sub-Task A.4.2

ADMINISTER MEDICATION AND/OR PROCEDURES.

Required skills and abilities	Required core knowledge
ECEs are able to:	*ECEs know:*
a) obtain written instructions and permission from parents;	1) federal/provincial/territorial/municipal regulations and quality standards;
b) read labels and administer prescribed medications accurately;	2) program policy for storing and administering medication;
c) record dispensing/administering and intake of medication;	3) specialized equipment and procedures for individual children;
d) use specialized medical equipment (e.g., asthma masks, catheters, feeding tubes);	4) signs and symptoms of allergic and adverse reactions.
e) ensure a daily follow-up with parents regarding the dosage of medication administered to the child during the day;	
f) document medication and procedures.	

Sub-Task A.4.3

IMPLEMENT PREVENTATIVE HEALTH AND SAFETY MEASURES.

Required skills and abilities	Required core knowledge
ECEs are able to:	*ECEs know:*
a) sterilize and sanitize play materials and equipment;	1) sanitization and sterilization regulations;
b) use universal hand washing/sanitizing procedures;	2) communicable diseases and program policies;
c) recognize signs of various communicable diseases;	3) universal precautions (e.g., hand washing, handling of body fluids);
d) notify parents/families/health departments of communicable disease outbreak, as required;	4) professional sources (e.g., books, publications, reputable Internet sites) and quality standards and practices;
e) implement exclusion policy, as required;	5) food safety practices.
f) conduct a daily health check of each child;	
g) recognize the effect of personal health on the well-being of the children.	

Sub-Task A.4.4

DEVELOP AND IMPLEMENT SAFE TRAVELLING PRACTICES.

Required skills and abilities	Required core knowledge
ECEs are able to:	*ECEs know:*
a) transport children using safe practices and CSA-approved equipment;	1) federal/provincial/territorial regulations;
b) follow guidelines for stroller use;	2) quality standards and practices;
c) promote street safety;	3) safety policies of the program;
d) promote and educate children about transportation safety;	4) developmentally-appropriate transportation;
e) meet provincial/territorial transportation requirements;	5) appropriate safety equipment.
f) complete and identify safety checklists;	
g) use developmentally-appropriate transportation (e.g., strollers, car seats, bikes, wagons);	
h) use appropriate safety equipment (e.g., helmets, seat belts);	
i) take precautions when planning and implementing field trips and celebrations (e.g., pre-trip visits, consideration of transportation issues).	

Sub-Task A.4.5

PROVIDE FIRST AID AND CPR.

Required skills and abilities	Required core knowledge
ECEs are able to:	*ECEs know:*
a) identify when first aid and CPR is required;	1) current first aid and CPR practices.
b) maintain certification;	
c) administer first aid and CPR.	

Sub-Task A.4.6

IMPLEMENT EMERGENCY AND EVACUATION PLANS.

Required skills and abilities	Required core knowledge
ECEs are able to:	*ECEs know:*
a) identify emergency situations;	1) emergency and evacuation plans;
b) keep plans up-to-date;	2) federal/provincial/territorial/municipal regulations;
c) educate children and families about the plans;	3) quality standards and practices;
d) practice safety procedures regularly;	4) contact information for emergency services personnel.
e) keep children's emergency contact information up-to-date and accessible;	
f) record/document and report practices and drills, as required;	
g) respond to emergencies (e.g., tornadoes, hurricanes, snowstorms, extreme heat, floods, chemical spills, power outages);	
h) contact appropriate emergency departments when necessary (e.g., fire, police, ambulance).	

Sub-Task A.4.7

IMPLEMENT SECURITY PROCEDURES.

Required skills and abilities	Required core knowledge
ECEs are able to:	*ECEs know:*
a) ensure security procedures are followed (e.g., lockdown, serious occurrence procedures, intrusion procedures);	1) security procedures of the program;
	2) quality standards and practices;
b) ensure security procedures are visible;	3) provincial/territorial/municipal regulations.
c) operate security equipment (e.g., alarms, locks).	

Sub-Task A.4.8

REVIEW SAFETY-RELATED ISSUES.

Required skills and abilities	Required core knowledge
ECEs are able to:	*ECEs know:*
a) keep abreast and respond to safety-related information (e.g., product recalls, safety bulletins);	1) professional sources (e.g., books, publications, reputable Internet sites) and quality standards and practices;
b) identify, address and report unsafe equipment, materials, food, practices, policies and procedures;	2) safety-related resources (e.g., websites, agencies, publications);
c) debrief and evaluate responses to safety issues and make warranted changes, as required;	3) related regulations, standards of practice and licensing requirements.
d) appropriately relay safety concerns.	

Sub-Task A.4.9

FOLLOW SAFE TOILETING AND DIAPERING PROCEDURES.

Required skills and abilities	Required core knowledge
ECEs are able to: a) implement developmentally-appropriate diapering procedures; b) ensure sanitary conditions are always maintained; c) use proper diaper-handling and disposal procedures; d) use safe lifting procedures; e) promote self-help skills as children are ready; f) supervise children; g) work collaboratively with parents to ensure consistency; h) effectively communicate with parents and children; i) document and report.	*ECEs know:* 1) health regulations; 2) cultural expectations from parents; 3) quality standards and practices; 4) child development theories.

Sub-Task A.4.10

IDENTIFY AND REPORT SUSPECTED CASES OF CHILD ABUSE AND NEGLECT.

Required skills and abilities	Required core knowledge
ECEs are able to:	*ECEs know:*
a) identify and document signs of abuse and neglect;	1) signs of abuse and neglect;
b) maintain confidentiality to protect the child and family while addressing the situation appropriately;	2) legislation regarding duty to report;
c) follow proper protocols for reporting abuse and neglect;	3) procedures for reporting abuse and neglect;
d) inform parents about Canadian legislation and program expectations of behavioural guidance and the rights of the child;	4) policies of confidentiality;
e) keep lines of communication open with families.	5) community agencies to support families;
	6) children's rights.

Sub-Task A.4.11

PROMOTE A HEALTHY LIFESTYLE.

Required skills and abilities	Required core knowledge
ECEs are able to:	*ECEs know:*
a) promote and model good hygiene habits;	1) relaxation techniques;
b) promote and model physical exercise;	2) professional literature and quality standards;
c) promote and model healthy eating habits;	3) hygiene measures;
d) promote need for adequate sleep and naptime schedules;	4) strategies for children's health;
e) promote children's physical and mental health;	5) child's family and personal circumstances.
f) help the children to develop relaxation techniques;	
g) collaborate with other professionals and agencies to enhance health in the program;	
h) provide opportunities for outdoor activities every day;	
i) support parents in keeping a balanced home life that will promote a balanced environment for their children.	

Sub-Task A.4.12

PROMOTE ENVIRONMENTALLY-SOUND PRACTICES.

Required skills and abilities	Required core knowledge
ECEs are able to:	*ECEs know:*
a) educate self about environmentally-sound alternatives;	1) environmentally-sound options;
b) plan, program and implement environmentally-sound activities;	2) emerging quality standards and practices;
c) promote and involve parents in environmentally-sound activities within the program;	3) organizational policies and procedures.
d) use environmentally-sound supplies and materials.	

Sub-Task A.4.13

ACTIVELY SUPERVISE CHILDREN.

Required skills and abilities	Required core knowledge
ECEs are able to: a) position themselves to maximize their view of areas; b) scan facilities frequently to maintain awareness of space and the group dynamic; c) recognize when redirection and intervention is required; d) maintain child-staff ratios; e) anticipate and communicate transition times; f) record and communicate ongoing number of children; g) work collaboratively with team members; h) create environments that do not impede supervision; i) engage children and facilitate play appropriately.	ECEs know: 1) supervision practices; 2) staff-child ratios; 3) environment rating scales; 4) safety checklists; 5) child guidance strategies (e.g., engagement, facilitation); 6) quality standards and practices.

Sub-Task A.4.14

SUPERVISE CHILDREN DURING OUTINGS AND FIELD TRIPS.

Required skills and abilities	Required core knowledge
ECEs are able to:	*ECEs know:*
a) ensure all emergency contact information for children, medication, first aid supplies and communication devices (e.g., cell phones) are on-hand;	1) environment and location that they will be visiting (e.g., potential allergens, hazards);
b) enhance ratios, when possible;	2) supervision practices;
c) assign designated persons (e.g., staff, parents, volunteers) to groups of children;	3) safety practices and procedures;
d) meet transportation requirements;	4) federal/provincial/territorial and program transportation requirements;
e) implement inclusion practices to ensure all children can participate in outings and field trips.	5) quality standards and practices.

Task A.5

Meet nutritional needs.

Context Statement:

Early Childhood Educators may plan and provide nutritious meals and snacks and promote and demonstrate healthy eating habits for children. They may be responsible for the preparation of food and for the nutrition of children of varying ages and with various dietary needs and considerations. ECEs follow health and safety precautions and safe food-handling practices in the preparation and provision of food.

Sub-Task A.5.1

PLAN AND PROVIDE NUTRITIOUS MEALS AND SNACKS.

Required skills and abilities	Required core knowledge
ECEs are able to:	*ECEs know:*
a) show an interest in and provide varied and nutritious types of food;	1) *Canada's Food Guide* and *Food Guide for First Nations, Inuit and Métis;*
b) follow *Canada's Food Guide* and *Food Guide for First Nations, Inuit and Métis;*	2) public health laws and regulations;
c) develop and prepare balanced meals;	3) cooking techniques and safe food-handling practices;
d) promote culinary activities with the children;	4) nutritional value of the various types of food;
e) adapt menus and meals to the age group, culture, needs, portion sizes, etc.;	5) developmental nutritional needs and children's preferences;
f) respect any food restrictions (e.g., allergies, intolerances, vegan and vegetarian diets);	6) vegetarian/vegan diets.
g) respect and respond to family dietary practices;	
h) integrate cultural nutrition practices;	
i) follow food safety principles and rules.	

Sub-Task A.5.2

PREPARE AND PROVIDE INFANT NUTRITION.

Required skills and abilities	Required core knowledge
ECEs are able to:	*ECEs know:*
a) follow the parents' plan for feeding, including food introduction;	1) policies and procedures of the program;
b) serve food in safe conditions (e.g., milk and food temperature);	2) public health laws and child care regulations;
c) adhere to the baby's biological clock (i.e., feeding according to baby's hunger);	3) food-preparation techniques (e.g., formula preparation);
d) adapt menus and meals to the infant's stage of development;	4) nutritional value of the various types of food;
e) pay attention to any food restrictions (e.g., allergies, intolerances);	5) safety measures;
f) preserve nutritional integrity of foods (e.g., proper cooking, preparing, heating and storage procedures);	6) bottle-feeding procedures
g) facilitate the transition between breastfeeding/bottle and solid foods;	
h) encourage the bond with the infant through feeding and holding.	

Sub-Task A.5.3

PROMOTE HEALTHY EATING.

Required skills and abilities	Required core knowledge
ECEs are able to:	*ECEs know:*
a) show a positive attitude and take positive forms of action (e.g., show respect for the child's appetite, rhythm and tastes);	1) *Canada's Food Guide* and *Food Guide for First Nations, Inuit and Métis;*
b) develop individualized and positive strategies;	2) public health laws and regulations;
c) promote an environment that is conducive to healthy eating;	3) cooking techniques;
d) follow *Canada's Food Guide* and *Food Guide for First Nations, Inuit and Métis;*	4) nutritional value of the various types of food;
e) provide parents with information about nutritious and safe food choices;	5) quality standards and practices;
f) keep parents informed about child's food intake;	6) eating habits and issues based on individual child's age, development and cultural diversity.
g) apply health and safety principles and rules;	
h) use mealtime as an opportunity for learning about healthy eating;	
i) create a positive social and emotional atmosphere at mealtimes;	
j) incorporate dietary diversities.	

Sub-Task A.5.4

ACCOMMODATE FOR SPECIAL NUTRITIONAL REQUIREMENTS.

Required skills and abilities	Required core knowledge
ECEs are able to: a) obtain information from the family about any specific nutritional needs for the child; b) post and adhere to any specific nutritional requirements for the child; c) make all of the children aware of any specific food requirements and safety rules (e.g., allergies, food restrictions); d) acknowledge cultural needs and traditions in menu planning and food preparation.	*ECEs know:* 1) cultural diversity, food restrictions and allergies; 2) nutritional requirements of various age groups; 3) child development theories.

| Task A.6 | **Guide children's behaviour.** |

Context Statement:

Early Childhood Educators use a variety of behaviour guidance techniques that are proactive and appropriate to the ages and stages of development, recognizing individual competency of children to positively guide behaviour.

Sub-Task A.6.1

ESTABLISH AN ENVIRONMENT TO FOSTER POSITIVE BEHAVIOUR IN THE PROGRAM.

Required skills and abilities	Required core knowledge
ECEs are able to:	*ECEs know:*
a) select guidance strategies based on: • observations; • developmental needs of the child; • interests of the child; • community resources; • philosophy of program; b) incorporate parents' expectations for their child's behaviour; c) create an emotional bond with the child based on social and emotional needs; d) engage in reflective practice; e) arrange the environment to suit the child's needs and interests; f) create play areas that are compatible with one another (e.g., quiet play versus active play); g) establish play areas that address the needs of all children and their overall development; h) make materials available to the child.	1) child development theories; 2) program and room-planning techniques; 3) professional sources (e.g., books, publications, reputable Internet sites) and quality standards and practices; 4) organizational philosophy.

Sub-Task A.6.2

GUIDE AND OBSERVE CHILDREN.

Required skills and abilities	Required core knowledge
ECEs are able to:	*ECEs know:*
a) engage with the child (e.g., interact with the child at eye level);	1) observation methods and tools;
b) use observation tools;	2) individual child's behaviour;
c) ask open-ended questions;	3) individual child's skills.
d) interpret results of observations and respond;	
e) provide active learning activities;	
f) share observations with parents and colleagues;	
g) document behaviour frequency, duration and types.	

Sub-Task A.6.3

IMPLEMENT POSITIVE BEHAVIOUR GUIDANCE.

Required skills and abilities	Required core knowledge
ECEs are able to:	*ECEs know:*
a) build positive, trusting relationship with the child;	1) conflict resolution approaches;
b) model positive social skills;	2) democratic intervention approaches;
c) observe children to identify possible reasons for behaviour;	3) observation methods and tools.
d) use positive language when responding to the child's behaviour;	
e) act consistently and positively (e.g., follow through with expectations for individual children within the program);	
f) establish behavioural management methods that are consistently applied by all staff;	
g) identify needs of the child;	
h) facilitate patterns of interactions (i.e., social dynamics of the group);	
i) provide clear directions (e.g., use positive voice tone and body language);	
j) recognize effects of physical environment, schedules and routines on behaviour;	
k) establish and model conflict resolution methods;	
l) give the child strategies to develop self-control and self-regulation;	
m) reinforce positive behaviour;	
n) promote self-esteem;	
o) foster development of the child's autonomy;	
p) involve the parent in the process, as needed, to promote change.	

Sub-Task A.6.4

FACILITATE APPROPRIATE LANGUAGE.

Required skills and abilities	Required core knowledge
ECEs are able to:	*ECEs know:*
a) help the child to verbalize their feelings and needs and expand their current vocabulary;	1) communication methods;
b) listen actively to the child's language;	2) language used in the home.
c) recognize and reformulate the child's vocabulary;	
d) use an appropriate linguistic model (e.g., vocabulary, syntax).	

Sub-Task A.6.5

FACILITATE CONFLICT RESOLUTION.

Required skills and abilities	Required core knowledge
ECEs are able to:	*ECEs know:*
a) properly decode the verbal and non-verbal codes and cues used by the child;	1) cultural codes and cues;
b) listen to the child;	2) conflict resolution methods.
c) place themselves at the child's level and maintain visual contact;	
d) show respect for the child's emotions expressed or suppressed;	
e) provide a positive setting;	
f) promote the child's autonomy.	

Sub-Task A.6.6

FACILITATE EMPATHY.

Required skills and abilities	Required core knowledge
ECEs are able to:	*ECEs know:*
a) reflect the child's emotions;	1) cultural and physical differences.
b) make comforting gestures;	
c) facilitate discussion of differences (e.g., family composition, physical abilities, sexual orientation, cultural holidays) with the child;	
d) demonstrate empathy.	

Sub-Task A.6.7

USE AND PROMOTE ACTIVE LISTENING SKILLS.

Required skills and abilities	Required core knowledge
ECEs are able to:	*ECEs know:*
a) demonstrate openness and availability to the child;	1) active listening skills.
b) reformulate the child's emotions and needs;	
c) provide one-on-one moments with the child;	
d) encourage the children to listen to one another (e.g., speaking at the appropriate time in discussions).	

Sub-Task A.6.8

USE NATURAL OR LOGICAL CONSEQUENCES.

Required skills and abilities	Required core knowledge
ECEs are able to:	ECEs know:
a) observe and intervene consistently in dealing with the child's actions;	1) child development theories;
b) apply consequences while respecting the child's development;	2) the child's individual development;
c) take follow-up action;	3) meaning of natural and logical consequences.
d) act on the basis of clear, constant, consistent, concrete and appropriate limits;	
e) ensure the team is consistent in their practices.	

Sub-Task A.6.9

PROTECT CHILDREN FROM PHYSICAL AND EMOTIONAL HARM.

Required skills and abilities	Required core knowledge
ECEs are able to:	*ECEs know:*
a) ensure the working environment is safe;	1) safety measures, laws and regulations;
b) follow the standards for outdoor facilities;	2) child development theories.
c) ensure equipment and materials are suited to the age level;	
d) ensure the children have clear instructions;	
e) apply a code of conduct to prevent physical and psychological violence.	

Sub-Task A.6.10

FACILITATE PROBLEM-SOLVING SKILLS.

Required skills and abilities	Required core knowledge
ECEs are able to:	*ECEs know:*
a) introduce problem-solving strategies appropriate to the age group and environment;	1) problem-solving techniques;
b) lead the child to think and come up with their own solutions that are age appropriate;	2) democratic intervention techniques.
c) encourage the child's self-sufficiency by guiding them in learning how to solve problems;	
d) demonstrate flexibility and creativity in order to adapt to situations;	
e) respect the child's responses and choices;	
f) provide a safe environment while the child works towards solutions to their problems;	
g) share power between staff and children.	

Sub-Task A.6.11

FACILITATE COPING SKILLS.

Required skills and abilities	Required core knowledge
ECEs are able to: a) treat each child as unique; b) create a significant link with the children; c) respect and respond to the children's needs; d) give the children the opportunity to bring a transitional object; e) prepare the group to receive a new child; f) encourage the gradual integration of the new child in the environment; g) promote collaboration among the parent, the child and the educator; h) welcome and integrate the family into the environment; i) engage children in discussions regarding issues of change (e.g., new baby, moving); j) demonstrate adaptability and flexibility; k) create a welcoming and safe environment.	ECEs know: 1) ecological approach (e.g., child surrounded by significant people, peers, family members and service organizations); 2) signs and symptoms of child stress.

SECTION B
EQUIPMENT AND FACILITIES

Task B.1	Develop and maintain a safe environment.

Context Statement:

Early Childhood Educators perform regular equipment and facilities inspections, monitor and perform minor maintenance activities, and follow health and safety practices to develop and maintain a safe environment for children.

Sub-Task B.1.1
CHECK FOR PHYSICAL HAZARDS.

Required skills and abilities	Required core knowledge
ECEs are able to: a) inspect play materials, equipment and environment (both indoors and outdoors); b) address and remove any physical hazards.	*ECEs know:* 1) developmentally-appropriate play materials and equipment; 2) potential hazards.

Sub-Task B.1.2

MAINTAIN AND IMPLEMENT SAFETY STANDARDS AND PROTOCOLS.

Required skills and abilities	Required core knowledge
ECEs are able to:	ECEs know:
a) perform inspections by completing checklists and forms;	1) safety standards as per provincial/territorial regulations;
b) consider developmental needs and abilities of all children within the group;	2) child development theories;
c) follow safety procedures and policies;	3) related regulations, standards of practice and licensing requirements.
d) record issues, concerns and incidents and report when necessary.	

Sub-Task B.1.3

USE DEVELOPMENTALLY-APPROPRIATE EQUIPMENT.

Required skills and abilities	Required core knowledge
ECEs are able to:	*ECEs know:*
a) identify developmentally-appropriate equipment;	1) curriculum theories;
b) make informed equipment choices to prepare balanced learning environments;	2) skills and abilities of children;
c) observe and evaluate the use of the equipment;	3) child development theories;
d) make equipment purchase recommendations.	4) interests of children.

Sub-Task B.1.4

ADAPT PROGRAMMING AND EQUIPMENT TO UNIQUE SETTINGS AND SITUATIONS.

Required skills and abilities	Required core knowledge
ECEs are able to:	*ECEs know:*
a) find creative means to meet the development needs and interests of the children; b) be flexible, responsive and proactive.	1) child development theories; 2) different learning styles and skill mastery; 3) professional sources (e.g., books, publications, community resources) and quality standards and practices.

Task B.2

Operate and maintain facilities.

Context Statement:

Early Childhood Educators create and maintain indoor and outdoor physical and learning environments that promote the health, safety and well-being of children and adults. ECEs rotate indoor and outdoor play materials and equipment, maintain inventories of equipment and supplies and regularly monitor the safety of the environment and materials.

Sub-Task B.2.1

MAINTAIN EQUIPMENT, MATERIALS AND FURNISHINGS.

Required skills and abilities	Required core knowledge
ECEs are able to:	*ECEs know:*
a) maintain safe play materials and equipment;	1) developmentally-appropriate theories and equipment.
b) follow directions and instructions for use;	
c) maintain a sense of order so that materials are found easily and injuries are prevented (e.g., tripping);	
d) assemble and disassemble equipment;	
e) assess priorities for children and program;	
f) research and source equipment;	
g) plan and prepare supplies for activities;	
h) maintain adequate inventory.	

Sub-Task B.2.2

MAINTAIN INDOOR AND OUTDOOR PHYSICAL ENVIRONMENT.

Required skills and abilities	Required core knowledge
ECEs are able to:	*ECEs know:*
a) identify any physical hazards;	1) health and safety protocols and procedures;
b) document and report major concerns;	2) federal/provincial/territorial regulations and requirements (e.g., CSA);
c) control/maintain adequate noise, temperature, air quality and humidity levels;	3) importance of components of the environment and their impact on children (e.g., natural light, views of the outdoors, natural materials, different colours and textures, soft furnishings);
d) properly store hazardous substances;	
e) solve minor issues;	
f) conduct daily playground safety checks prior to playground use;	4) outdoor safety protocols and procedures;
g) maintain safety standards;	5) related regulations, standards of practice and licensing regulations (e.g., playground safety).
h) maintain cleanliness of outdoor facilities;	
i) ensure walkways, play areas, paths, driveways and doorways are clear and free of hazards;	
j) take action, as necessary (e.g., remove unsafe equipment).	

Sub-Task B.2.3

MONITOR CLEANLINESS AND SANITATION OF ALL AREAS USED BY CHILDREN.

Required skills and abilities	Required core knowledge
ECEs are able to:	*ECEs know:*
a) identify areas that need to be cleaned;	1) cleaning and sanitary practices;
b) follow health and hygiene standards issued by the government and licensing authorities;	2) regulations and requirements (e.g., federal/provincial/territorial/municipal, Occupational Health and Safety Act).
c) control and prevent the spread of communicable illnesses and infections;	
d) check play materials and equipment to ensure cleanliness and sanitation;	
e) properly store hazardous substances;	
f) read and interpret step-by-step instructions;	
g) follow hygiene and cleanliness procedures, as required;	
h) communicate concerns and actions with the early childhood team.	

SECTION C
FAMILY AND COMMUNITY RELATIONS

Task C.1	**Form collaborative partnerships with families.**

Context Statement:

Early Childhood Educators form collaborative partnerships with children's families that honour their role as the child's primary caregiver, respect their parenting practices, and provide meaningful opportunities for families to determine their children's early learning and care experiences. ECEs adapt their programs to the needs of diverse families, respecting each family's composition, language and culture. They help connect families with needed resources, furthering the child's healthy development and learning.

Sub-Task C.1.1

BUILD AND MAINTAIN MEANINGFUL RELATIONSHIPS WITH FAMILIES.

Required skills and abilities	Required core knowledge
ECEs are able to:	*ECEs know:*
a) empathize with parents;	1) appropriate social interaction skills;
b) communicate ongoing successes and concerns;	2) inclusive practices (e.g., different family structures, cultural practices);
c) discuss program and individual needs;	3) challenges facing families (e.g., shift-work, income disparity, rural/urban);
d) discuss expectations;	4) quality standards and practices;
e) respect that parents are the experts on their own children;	5) the distinction between the role of the ECE and the parent;
f) seek out additional information to assist in understanding parents and families;	6) philosophy of the program.
g) respect different family structures (e.g., same sex, single parent);	
h) create a welcoming environment for all families;	
i) encourage input from parents in developing individual plans or addressing concerns as they arise.	

Sub-Task C.1.2

ORIENT FAMILIES TO THE PROGRAM.

Required skills and abilities	Required core knowledge
ECEs are able to:	*ECEs know:*
a) discuss goals and objectives of the program;	1) related regulations, standards of practice and licensing requirements;
b) discuss program philosophy, policies, procedures, expectations and daily routines before child enters the program;	2) organizational values, policies and procedures.
c) explain orientation process and materials;	
d) solicit information and answer questions from families about their children;	
e) discuss considerations for the individual child;	
f) discuss transition plan for bringing the child into the program and any planned changes that will impact the child;	
g) consider the family's needs, cultural and/or religious practices and preferences related to childrearing	
h) consider the family's goals for the child upon entrance into and duration in the program;	
i) modify routines, foods and activities (to the extent possible) to reflect and respect family practices and preferences.	

Sub-Task C.1.3

COMMUNICATE WITH FAMILIES.

Required skills and abilities	Required core knowledge
ECEs are able to:	*ECEs know:*
a) use a variety of communication strategies (e.g., invitations to program activities, newsletters, bulletins, notices, websites);	1) quality standards and practices;
b) provide families with information about significant proposed changes or decisions that may affect them or their children and ensures that families are informed when there are changes in policies or procedures;	2) effective communication strategies; 3) organizational philosophy, values, policies and procedures; 4) needs of families.
c) give parents opportunities to provide their input;	
d) continuously engage the family in information-sharing about the child's daily experiences.	

Sub-Task C.1.4

COLLABORATE WITH PARENTS.

Required skills and abilities	Required core knowledge
ECEs are able to:	*ECEs know:*
a) involve the family in identifying and achieving expectations for the child;	1) observation methods and tools;
b) nurture parents as advocates for their children;	2) availability of resources and support agencies;
c) conduct parent conferences to review progress;	3) interpersonal communication techniques.
d) respond promptly when concerns are expressed;	
e) explore and consider options when differences of opinion occur;	
f) obtain required permission from parent for resource support;	
g) work with other professionals to support children and families seeking information and resources;	
h) identify and recommend community resources available to children and their families;	
i) demonstrate understanding of their roles as advocates for children, families and their communities.	

Sub-Task C.1.5

PROVIDE FAMILY RESOURCES.

Required skills and abilities	Required core knowledge
ECEs are able to:	*ECEs know:*
a) carry out survey of needs and wants of parents;	1) research methods;
b) suggest and solicit topics for resources (e.g., workshops, newsletters, bulletin boards);	2) family needs;
c) research topics for resources;	3) presentation and facilitation techniques.
d) advise parents of resources through newsletters, memos, postings, parent boards, etc.;	
e) engage 'experts' on topics or facilitate workshops.	

Task C.2

Use community resources.

Context Statement:

Early Childhood Educators establish relationships with and use the resources of the children's communities to support the achievement of program objectives, including the establishment of reciprocal relationships with agencies that support goals for curriculum, health promotion, children's transitions, inclusion and diversity. ECEs must possess a familiarity with the resources available within their communities and network with these resources to form partnerships and develop awareness programs.

Sub-Task C.2.1

ACCESS AND ENGAGE COMMUNITY RESOURCES, FACILITIES AND SERVICES.

Required skills and abilities	Required core knowledge
ECEs are able to:	*ECEs know:*
a) collect information on the resources in the area;	1) resources, facilities and services within the area;
b) post contact information for families;	2) program, families and children's needs.
c) identify community affiliations of the program and staff;	
d) identify potential community partners;	
e) utilize community facilities and services (e.g., libraries, parks);	
f) recruit resources;	
g) network with community members to implement programs and develop partnerships;	
h) maintain positive partnerships;	
i) communicate effectively.	

Sub-Task C.2.2

RAISE AWARENESS OF COMMUNITY EVENTS.

Required skills and abilities	Required core knowledge
ECEs are able to:	*ECEs know:*
a) encourage parents to get involved and participate in community events;	1) demographics and needs of the community.
b) demonstrate enthusiasm for program and related organizations (e.g., at booths and kiosks);	
c) advocate for programs, organizations and professions that are concerned with the development of families using the program.	

Sub-Task C.2.3

INVOLVE VOLUNTEERS.

Required skills and abilities	Required core knowledge
ECEs are able to:	*ECEs know:*
a) orient volunteers to the program (e.g., parents, students, family members);	1) related regulations, standards of practice and licensing requirements.
b) assign tasks to volunteers;	
c) build relationships with volunteers;	
d) adhere to organizational policies and procedures for volunteers.	

Task C.3

Advocate for children and families.

Context Statement:

Early Childhood Educators advocate for children and their families by establishing ties between parents and various resources and by advocating for support from governmental agencies and associations. They identify the needs of children and families through clear communication of accurate information.

Sub-Task C.3.1

MAKE CONNECTIONS BETWEEN FAMILIES AND RESOURCES.

Required skills and abilities	Required core knowledge
ECEs are able to:	*ECEs know:*
a) collaborate with parents to identify needs of children and family dynamics;	1) their roles and responsibilities and those of others in the program setting;
b) advocate on behalf of families;	2) availability of resources and organizations.
c) collaborate and plan with outside agencies;	
d) promote awareness to parents and families;	
e) provide information on resources, as required;	
f) exhibit confidence when presenting a message;	
g) sensitively communicate with families;	
h) support parents when requested.	

Sub-Task C.3.2

RESPECT THE RIGHTS OF THE CHILD.

Required skills and abilities	Required core knowledge
ECEs are able to: a) ensure families' cultural practices, traditions and home language(s) are respected in practice and policy; b) provide children with meaningful and developmentally-appropriate opportunities to express their views; c) ensure children's opinions and views are listened to by the adults in a respectful manner; d) encourage children to respect the rights of others, cooperate with each other, consider the views of others in a respectful fashion and honour diversity; e) recognize when children's rights have been violated and take appropriate action.	*ECEs know:* 1) children's rights as outlined in *United Nations' Convention on the Rights of the Child;* 2) program policies regarding the rights of children; 3) standards of practice and laws.

Task C.4

Provide an inclusive environment.

Context Statement:

Early Childhood Educators provide an inclusive environment for children and families through the integration and acceptance of unique and diverse familial and cultural realities. ECEs also ensure the acceptance and complete inclusion of children with special needs through program modification and the development of inclusion plans.

Sub-Task C.4.1

COLLABORATE WITH PARENTS TO IDENTIFY STRENGTHS, NEEDS AND INTERESTS OF THE CHILD.

Required skills and abilities	Required core knowledge
ECEs are able to:	*ECEs know:*
a) obtain information about strengths, needs and interests of the children when they register and on an ongoing basis;	1) individual children and their families;
b) plan meetings with families to discuss their children's strengths and needs;	2) interpersonal communications techniques;
	3) observation methods and tools;
c) respect and include the family when planning special events;	4) value of diversity;
	5) the child's immediate environment, as well as the broader physical, socioeconomic and cultural context in which the family lives;
d) demonstrate empathy.	6) availability of community resources.

Sub-Task C.4.2

COLLABORATE WITH PARENTS AND OTHER PROFESSIONALS TO DEVELOP AND IMPLEMENT INCLUSION PLANS.

Required skills and abilities	Required core knowledge
ECEs are able to:	*ECEs know:*
a) establish a partnership with the professionals;	1) availability of professional services;
b) engage in active listening;	2) how to prepare a development support plan.
c) implement recommendations;	
d) attend meetings and take follow-up action;	
e) demonstrate adaptability and flexibility;	
f) work with team to prepare a development support plan.	

SECTION D
PROFESSIONAL RELATIONSHIPS

Task D.1	Work as a member of a team.

Context Statement:

Early Childhood Educators work as members of teams to develop learning environments that meet the needs of all children, staff and families. They establish and maintain relationships that support productive work and meet professional needs, recognize and capitalize on the strengths of fellow team members, share a vision and goal for their work, and provide mutual support, collaboration and assistance. These teams may include teachers, social workers, speech language pathologists, occupational therapists, physiotherapists, psychologists and other community practitioners.

Sub-Task D.1.1

CREATE PARTNERSHIPS WITH COLLEAGUES.

Required skills and abilities	Required core knowledge
ECEs are able to:	ECEs know:
a) demonstrate integrity in all professional relationships;	1) roles and responsibilities of self and others;
b) support colleagues and work collaboratively as a team through effective communication strategies;	2) Code of Ethics; 3) effective communication skills;
c) make time for discussion with co-workers;	4) conflict resolution skills;
d) be non-judgemental;	5) importance of creating a positive team environment.
e) offer assistance when needed;	
f) share resources and responsibilities;	
g) recognize strengths and limitations of self and co-workers;	
h) support colleagues to complete their work duties.	

Sub-Task D.1.2

PARTICIPATE IN MEETINGS.

Required skills and abilities	Required core knowledge
ECEs are able to:	*ECEs know:*
a) be prepared for meetings;	1) the issues at hand;
b) contribute to the development of a meeting agenda;	2) standard meeting protocols;
c) express ideas and concerns clearly and concisely and stay on topic;	3) conflict resolution skills;
d) engage in active listening;	4) their roles and responsibilities and those of team members;
e) respect the opinions of others;	5) positive communication techniques.
f) demonstrate positive communication skills;	
g) contribute to discussions and share information;	
h) resolve interpersonal conflicts and differences in a respectful manner.	

Sub-Task D.1.3

LIAISE WITH STAKEHOLDERS.

Required skills and abilities	Required core knowledge
ECEs are able to:	*ECEs know:*
a) use effective communication skills;	1) availability of resources;
b) facilitate conflict resolution;	2) interprofessional and multigenerational issues;
c) develop an action plan;	3) child development theories;
d) document discussions or actions;	4) roles and responsibilities of other professionals.
e) share knowledge and opinions.	

Sub-Task D.1.4

DEMONSTRATE LEADERSHIP.

Required skills and abilities	Required core knowledge
ECEs are able to:	*ECEs know:*
a) offer solutions to issues;	1) team-building techniques;
b) demonstrate a positive attitude;	2) conflict-resolution skills.
c) use organizational skills;	
d) acknowledge the strengths of others;	
e) demonstrate initiative;	
f) delegate tasks.	

Sub-Task D.1.5

FOLLOW POLICIES AND PROCEDURES.

Required skills and abilities	Required core knowledge
ECEs are able to: a) provide input into the development of policies and procedures; b) familiarize self with existing policies and procedures; c) provide comments and feedback to policies and procedures; d) suggest potential policies and procedures for development.	*ECEs know:* 1) current legislation, policies and procedures; 2) policy development procedures.

Task D.2

Mentor others.

Context Statement:

Early Childhood Educators often act as mentors and informal advisors for fellow ECEs who are new to the profession, as well as for students of early childhood education programs completing their practicum placements. As mentors, they share their professional experiences, coach the practices of those they are mentoring and guide others with positive attitudes, patient demeanours and open-minds. ECEs serve as resource persons, role model best practices and foster a positive regard for their profession.

Sub-Task D.2.1

SUPPORT AND GUIDE COLLEAGUES AND STUDENTS.

Required skills and abilities	Required core knowledge
ECEs are able to:	*ECEs know:*
a) complete appropriate forms;	1) related regulations, standards of practice and licensing requirements;
b) observe the work of colleagues and students;	2) effective communication techniques;
c) provide positive and constructive feedback;	3) mentoring principles.
d) provide a welcoming environment;	
e) engage in active listening;	
f) role model positive behaviours;	
g) demonstrate leadership;	
h) provide assistance, as required.	

Sub-Task D.2.2

FACILITATE MENTEES' PROFESSIONAL DEVELOPMENT.

Required skills and abilities	Required core knowledge
ECEs are able to:	*ECEs know:*
a) be sensitive and empathetic;	1) quality standards and practices;
b) provide immediate feedback;	
c) observe work of the mentee;	
d) provide positive reinforcement;	
e) explain expectations;	
f) offer suggestions for improvement;	
g) facilitate self-evaluation;	
h) complete evaluation forms.	

Sub-Task D.2.3

ACT AS A RESOURCE.

Required skills and abilities	Required core knowledge
ECEs are able to:	*ECEs know:*
a) be non-judgemental;	1) related regulations, standards of practice and licensing requirements;
b) model positive behaviours;	2) organizational values, policies and procedures;
c) provide information to others;	3) community support systems and resources.
d) network with others.	

SECTION E
PERSONAL AND PROFESSIONAL DEVELOPMENT

Task E.1	**Conduct self professionally.**

Context Statement:

Early Childhood Educators demonstrate professionalism on the job by adhering to policies and procedures enforced by their facilities and regulatory bodies. They follow a Code of Ethics and maintain confidentiality to respect the rights of the children and families. ECEs conduct themselves in a professional manner by following dress codes, managing their time effectively and upholding required certifications and registrations.

Sub-Task E.1.1

MAINTAIN PROFESSIONALISM.

Required skills and abilities	Required core knowledge
ECEs are able to:	*ECEs know:*
a) maintain professional demeanour (e.g., dress appropriately, use appropriate tone of voice, be respectful of others, punctuality);	1) organization's expectations for professional conduct;
b) apply due diligence;	2) importance of being aware of their behaviours and attitudes when interacting with the public;
c) exhibit a non-judgemental attitude;	3) quality standards and practices.
d) be open-minded and accepting of constructive feedback;	
e) adhere to division of personal life and professional life.	

Sub-Task E.1.2

FOLLOW POLICIES AND PROCEDURES.

Required skills and abilities	Required core knowledge
ECEs are able to:	*ECEs know:*
a) adhere to various policies and procedures (e.g., public health policies, education and child care Acts, behaviour management policies);	1) organizational and regulatory body (e.g., provincial/ territorial) policies and procedures;
b) participate in the development of new policies and procedures;	2) quality standards and practices.
c) participate in the revision of existing policies and procedures;	
d) follow through when policies and procedures have been violated.	

Sub-Task E.1.3

USE A CODE OF ETHICS TO GUIDE PRACTICE.

Required skills and abilities	Required core knowledge
ECEs are able to:	*ECEs know:*
a) recognize and follow requirements outlined in an applicable Code of Ethics (e.g., program, association).	1) Code of Ethics.
b) apply ethical decision-making.	

Sub-Task E.1.4

MAINTAIN CONFIDENTIALITY.

Required skills and abilities	Required core knowledge
ECEs are able to:	*ECEs know:*
a) build trusting relationships with children and families;	1) federal/provincial/territorial privacy legislation;
b) respect the privacy of self and others;	2) importance of confidentiality.
c) share information on a 'need-to-know' basis;	
d) recognize consequences of breaching confidentiality.	

Sub-Task E.1.5

MAINTAIN REQUIRED PROFESSIONAL CERTIFICATIONS AND/OR REGISTRATIONS.

Required skills and abilities	Required core knowledge
ECEs are able to:	*ECEs know:*
a) participate in required training;	1) required professional certifications and/or registrations;
b) successfully complete required examinations;	2) other requirements according to provincial/territorial standards (e.g., first aid, CPR, WHMIS, medical certificates).
c) provide proof of certification and/or registration to employer.	

Sub-Task E.1.6

KEEP UP-TO-DATE WITH LEGISLATIVE REQUIREMENTS.

Required skills and abilities	Required core knowledge
ECEs are able to:	*ECEs know:*
a) keep abreast of changes to licensing and other legislated requirements;	1) provincial/territorial licensing and other legislated requirements.
b) communicate concerns related to licensing and other legislated requirements.	

Task E.2	**Maintain a work/life balance.**

Context Statement:

Early Childhood Educators must maintain a work/life balance to ensure that the stresses of work do not negatively impact their quality of life and health (both mental and physical). They must be able to acknowledge and work within their own professional and personal limitations.

Sub-Task E.2.1

ENGAGE IN ONGOING SELF-ASSESSMENT.

Required skills and abilities	**Required core knowledge**
ECEs are able to:	*ECEs know:*
a) assess personal physical and mental health;	1) signs and symptoms of fatigue and stress;
b) assess personal job satisfaction;	2) physical and emotional requirements of the profession.
c) accept advice;	
d) find solutions to issues and concerns;	
e) maintain a positive attitude.	

Sub-Task E.2.2

MAINTAIN PHYSICAL HEALTH.

Required skills and abilities	Required core knowledge
ECEs are able to:	*ECEs know:*
a) use proper lifting techniques;	1) requirements for annual medical care and immunizations;
b) recognize signs and symptoms of illness;	2) importance of personal health and safety;
c) recognize personal health limitations.	3) principles of ergonomics;
	4) their rights and responsibilities under health and safety legislation, labour standards legislation, and collective agreements.

Sub-Task E.2.3

MAINTAIN MENTAL WELL-BEING.

Required skills and abilities	Required core knowledge
ECEs are able to:	*ECEs know:*
a) regularly self-assess personal mental health;	1) available support services;
b) take breaks, scheduled vacations and sick leave, as required;	2) coping strategies;
c) utilize coping strategies;	3) their rights and responsibilities under health and safety legislation, labour standards legislation, and collective agreements;
d) recognize personal limits.	4) human resource policies of their organization.

Task E.3	**Participate in professional development.**

Context Statement:

Early Childhood Educators pursue, on an ongoing basis, the knowledge, skills and self-awareness needed to be professionally competent by participating in life-long professional development and continuous learning activities. They share and exchange ideas with their peers and fellow professionals to encourage collaboration to enhance recognition of and respect for their profession. ECEs engage in professional development activities to continually enhance the quality of their skills, knowledge and experience and the profession as a whole.

Sub-Task E.3.1

DEVELOP AND IMPLEMENT A PROFESSIONAL DEVELOPMENT PLAN.

Required skills and abilities	Required core knowledge
ECEs are able to:	*ECEs know:*
a) conduct a self-evaluation;	1) professional development activities and resources;
b) set goals and objectives;	2) methods for upgrading their knowledge and education.
c) source methods to achieve goals and objectives;	
d) set a timeframe for achieving goals and objectives;	
e) develop a plan for achieving goals and objectives;	
f) participate in goal-setting and decision-making.	

Sub-Task E.3.2
EVALUATE PROGRESS BASED ON THE PROFESSIONAL DEVELOPMENT PLAN.

Required skills and abilities	Required core knowledge
ECEs are able to:	*ECEs know:*
a) conduct a self-evaluation;	1) basic expectations of professional tasks;
b) receive feedback from team;	2) available professional and personal supports and resources;
c) monitor timelines;	3) reflective practice.
d) identify strengths and weaknesses;	
e) find solutions to problems;	
f) make revisions to professional development plan;	
g) use and promote reflective practice.	

Sub-Task E.3.3

PARTICIPATE IN PROFESSIONAL WORKSHOPS, COURSES AND ONGOING LEARNING.

Required skills and abilities	Required core knowledge
ECEs are able to:	*ECEs know:*
a) be receptive to new ideas;	1) reflective practice;
b) embrace learning opportunities;	2) importance of professional development;
c) actively participate in workshops and learning opportunities;	3) available professional development resources;
d) share learning outcomes and concepts with others (e.g., co-workers);	4) recertification requirements, where applicable.
e) read about and research new trends and concepts;	
f) seek professional development opportunities;	
g) create own professional development plan;	
h) research applicable professional development opportunities.	

Sub-Task E.3.4

NETWORK WITH PEERS.

Required skills and abilities	Required core knowledge
ECEs are able to:	*ECEs know:*
a) communicate verbally and in written form;	1) peer groups (e.g., colleagues, professional organizations, networks).
b) initiate conversations among internal and external peer groups;	
c) share ideas;	
d) engage in active listening;	
e) be receptive to new ideas;	
f) use technology to communicate with peer groups (e.g., online forums, email communication).	

Task E.4

Advocate for the profession.

Context Statement:

Early Childhood Educators advocate for the resources required to deliver quality programs by creating public awareness and obtaining recognition for their profession. They frequently distribute information about the profession in the form of written communication, open houses, seminars and presentations to educate the public and advocate for increased recognition and improved working conditions.

Sub-Task E.4.1
PARTICIPATE IN PROFESSIONAL ORGANIZATIONS.

Required skills and abilities	Required core knowledge
ECEs are able to:	*ECEs know:*
a) recognize value of affiliation with professional organizations (e.g., associations, unions);	1) membership requirements, benefits and expectations.
b) maintain professional memberships, as required;	
c) actively participate in professional organization activities;	
d) share ideas with other members.	

Sub-Task E.4.2
PROMOTE THE PROFESSION.

Required skills and abilities	Required core knowledge
ECEs are able to:	*ECEs know:*
a) build leadership capacity within the profession;	1) community demographics and needs.
b) share learning and knowledge;	
c) provide resources and informational materials;	
d) distribute promotional materials (e.g., flyers, posters);	
e) participate in outreach activities.	

SECTION F
RECORD KEEPING

Task F.1	**Maintain records for legislation and regulations.**

Context Statement:

Early Childhood Educators are required by provincial and territorial legislative and regulatory authorities to maintain records and documentation pertaining to activities and circumstances within their facilities and related to individual children. They must utilize effective documentation and filing skills to ensure that all pertinent and required information is recorded, submitted and filed according to established protocols. When required, ECEs may report activities and incidents related to individual children to parents.

Sub-Task F.1.1

RECORD DAILY AND MONTHLY ATTENDANCE.

Required skills and abilities	Required core knowledge
ECEs are able to:	*ECEs know:*
a) record time in and out;	1) related regulations, standards of practice and legislative requirements;
b) ensure sign-in of who drops off and picks up children, if required;	2) program policies and procedures.
c) record absences;	
d) document when children will leave and return to the program;	
e) file forms appropriately.	

Sub-Task F.1.2

RECORD AND REPORT ACCIDENTS, INCIDENTS AND OCCURRENCES, AS REQUIRED.

Required skills and abilities	Required core knowledge
ECEs are able to:	*ECEs know:*
a) complete appropriate forms;	1) related regulations, standards of practice and legislative requirements;
b) document and report specifics of accidents, incidents or occurrences, as required by own jurisdiction.	2) program policies and procedures.

Sub-Task F.1.3

RECORD CLEANING PROCEDURES.

Required skills and abilities	Required core knowledge
ECEs are able to:	*ECEs know:*
a) fill out forms as per legislated requirements;	1) related regulations, standards of practice and legislative requirements;
b) record cleaning of play materials, equipment, surfaces, materials and facilities.	2) program policies and procedures.

Sub-Task F.1.4

PREPARE RECORD OF ILL HEALTH.

Required skills and abilities	Required core knowledge
ECEs are able to:	*ECEs know:*
a) monitor and record symptoms of ill health;	1) related regulations, standards of practice and legislative requirements;
b) report ill health to parents;	2) signs and symptoms of ill health;
c) monitor and record absences due to communicable illnesses;	3) program policies and procedures.
d) inform relevant government agencies, as required.	

Sub-Task F.1.5

RECORD MEDICAL PROCEDURES AND THE ADMINISTRATION OF MEDICATION.

Required skills and abilities	Required core knowledge
ECEs are able to:	*ECEs know:*
a) record time and dosage of medication administered;	1) related regulations, standards of practice and legislative requirements;
b) record time and delivery of medical procedures;	2) program policies and procedures.
c) record observations according to policy.	

Sub-Task F.1.6

MAINTAIN UP-TO-DATE CHILDREN'S RECORDS.

Required skills and abilities	Required core knowledge
ECEs are able to:	*ECEs know:*
a) communicate regularly with parents to obtain up-to-date information; b) ensure all emergency contact details are current; c) ensure health and allergy information is current; d) obtain signed permission forms for various activities (e.g., photos field trips).	1) related regulations, standards of practice and legislative requirements; 2) program policies and procedures.

Sub-Task F.1.7

RECORD FACILITY MAINTENANCE AND SAFETY CHECKS.

Required skills and abilities	Required core knowledge
ECEs are able to:	*ECEs know:*
a) complete safety checks as per organizational policy; b) submit safety checks to appropriate authorities; c) follow up with concerns.	1) related regulations, standards of practice and legislative requirements; 2) program policies and procedures.

Sub-Task F.1.8

COMPLETE THE CHILD'S DAILY LOG FOR PARENTS.

Required skills and abilities	Required core knowledge
ECEs are able to: a) complete daily activity documentation (e.g., food intake, toileting/diapering, napping, unusual occurrences), as required by provincial/territorial legislation and policies.	*ECEs know:* 1) related regulations, standards of practice and legislative requirements; 2) program policies and procedures.

Sub-Task F.1.9

COMPLETE DAILY PROGRAM LOG BOOK/RECORD.

Required skills and abilities	Required core knowledge

ECEs are able to:
 	
a) record:
  • number of children in attendance;
  • safety drills;
  • medication administration;
  • special instructions for individual children;
  • visitors to the program;
 	
b) ensure log book/record is completed at the end of the day;
 	
c) ensure log book/record is read at the beginning of the day.
	ECEs know:
	
	1) related regulations, standards of practice and legislative requirements;
	
	2) program policies and procedures.

APPENDIX A
ACKNOWLEDGEMENTS

ACKNOWLEDGEMENTS

The Child Care Human Resources Sector Council wishes to express sincere appreciation to the many individuals who contributed, directly or indirectly, to this publication.

The sector council acknowledges the support and guidance of the Project Steering Committee Members:

Stephanie Seaman – Committee Chair
Chairperson –Early Childhood Educator
British Columbia Government and Service Employees'
Union / NUPGE
Community Social Services Component
Richmond, BC

Darcelle Cottons
Director
University of British Columbia Child Care Services
Vancouver, BC

Mary Goss-Prowse
Registrar of Child Care Services Certification
Association of Early Childhood Educators of NL
St. John's, NL

Karen Chandler
Professor
George Brown College
Toronto, ON

Gilles Cantin, Ph. D.
Professeur au département d'éducation et pédagogie
Université du Québec à Montréal
St-Jérôme, QC

Joanne Fournier
Enseignante en Techniques d'éducation à l'enfance
Cégep du Vieux Montréal
Montréal, QC

Melanie Dixon
Director of Professional Practice
College of Early Childhood Educators
Toronto, ON

Robin McMillan
Senior Consultant
Canadian Child Care Federation
Ottawa, ON

Helen Sinclair
Provincial Director of Child Care Services
Government of Newfoundland and Labrador
Representing P/T Directors of ECEC Working Groups
St. John's, NL

Child Care Human Resources Sector Council Staff:
Diana Carter, Executive Director
Kathryn Ohashi, Finance and Project Manager
Samantha Peek, Communications and Project Manager
Connie Brigham, Project Coordinator

Special acknowledgement is extended to the Occupational Standards Project Consultants Bernadette Allen and Kim Maclaren of Future Learning Inc., and the following representatives from the occupation:

Lina Al-habib	Chez moi des petits	Québec
Lisa Armstrong	Edward Jost Children's Centre	Nova Scotia
Sylvianne Arseneau	Garderie La Découverte	New Brunswick
Linda Arseneault	CCNB Campbellton	New Brunswick
Lisette Arseneau-Wedge	SEPENB	New Brunswick
Tim Baier	Alberta Child Care Association	Alberta
Natacha Bainbridge	Riverview Riddles and Rhymes	New Brunswick
Mary Baird	Abegweit First Nation Early Childhood Centre	Prince Edward Island
Ruth Bancroft	Langara Child Development Centre	British Columbia
Dorota Bartnik-Kapsa	UBC Child Care Summer of '73 Daycare	British Columbia
Athina Basiliadis	Glebe Parents' Daycare	Ontario
Karla Baxter Vincent	WES Center of Excellence - New Brunswick Community College	New Brunswick
Judy Beauchesne	Children's Choice Child Development Centre	Saskatchewan
April Bedard	Teen Parent Access to Education Society	Yukon Territory
Djaouida Belaissa	Ecole La Dauversiere "Sourire d'enfants"	Québec
Diane Bellesen	Family Child Care Provider	British Columbia
Mary Bennett	Cariboo Child Care Society	British Columbia
Andrea Bezanson	Mawiomi Child Care Centre	Nova Scotia
Roxanne Billard	Fisher Children's Centre	Newfoundland and Labrador
Sharon Black	Native Child and Family Services of Toronto	Ontario
Laurie Blackett	Funtimes Early Learning	Prince Edward Island
Nadine Blagdon	Kidcorp Learning Centre	Newfoundland and Labrador
Tami Brandrick	Parents' Child Development Co-operative	Saskatchewan
Crystal Brosseau-Lambert	Centre educatif La Clémentine	Ontario
Janice Brown	Little People's Workshop	Newfoundland and Labrador
Loretta Buckingham	Children's Circle Daycare	British Columbia
Florence Burdeny	Dauphin School Age Day Care Inc.	Manitoba
Jo-Ann Burkitt	Manitoba Child Care Program	Manitoba
Sylvette Burmeister	Champlain Daycare	Ontario
Carolyn Byers	North End Community Daycare Centre	Nova Scotia
Angie Calleberg	British Columbia Early Childhood Educator Registry	British Columbia
Randy Cameron	Glebe Parents' Daycare	Ontario
Sabine Cantave	CPP L'Étoile Filante	Ontario
Kim Carpenter	Parents' Child Development Co-operative	Saskatchewan
Lori Carson-Loveless	Kid's Korner Daycare and Montessori	New Brunswick
Jacqueline Chietera	CPE LA Barbouille	Québec
Mélanie Claudio	La Gribouille Cégep du Vieux Montréal	Québec
Rachel Clow	Tasiuqtigiit Society	Nunavut
Bettyanne Cole	Schoolhouse Playcare Centres of Durham - Altona Forest Location	Ontario

Wendy Cooper	West Wood Players Ltd.	British Columbia
Rose Ann Cotter	Capital Daycare	Ontario
Wendy Countaway	Jasper Place Child and Family Resource Centre	Alberta
Catherine Cross	Dartmouth Developmental Centre	Nova Scotia
France Cyr	Commission Scolaire Marguerite Bourgeoys	Québec
Julie Cyr	CISS - Children's Integration Support Services	Ontario
Nathalie Daigneault	CSMV	Québec
Sheila Davidson	Early Childhood Educators of British Columbia	British Columbia
Sue Delanoy	Communities for Children	Saskatchewan
Barbara Deschamp	Little People's Place Daycare	Nova Scotia
Julie Desroches	CPE Château des Neiges	Québec
Audrey Kathleen Didham	Kiddables Playschool Family Child Care	Newfoundland and Labrador
Maryline Dion	AFESEO	Ontario
Maryse Dion	Le Manège Kanata	Ontario
Kristen Doll	Sugar 'n Spice	Manitoba
Caroline Driedger	Kings Park Child Care	Manitoba
Jane Eaton	Janes Place Daycare	New Brunswick
Shawnda Farquhar	Unicorn Children's Centre	New Brunswick
Hélène Faye	Brin d'herbe	Ontario
Nicole Ferguson Marshall	SIAST - ECE	Saskatchewan
Jane Fisher	Just for You Children's Centre	Prince Edward Island
Janice Foote	Government of Nova Scotia - Department of Community Services	Nova Scotia
Brenda Frey	Dalhousie Parents' Daycare	Ontario
Isabelle Gagnon	Garderie Porte Soleil	Québec
Liane Gallop	Good Morning Creative Arts and Preschool	Ontario
Josée Gélinas	CPE a Tire d'Aile	Québec
Don Giesbrecht	Canadian Child Care Federation	Manitoba
Maria Gillis	Unicorn Children's Centre	New Brunswick
Kim Goerzen	Kings Park Child Care	Manitoba
Sister Celeste Goulet	Sister Celeste Child Development Centre	Northwest Territories
Donna Gruchy	Daybreak Parent Child Centre	Newfoundland and Labrador
Randi Gurholt-Seary	Canadian Union of Public Emplpoyees	British Columbia
Mariaflor S. Gutierrez	M&E Day Home	Alberta
Doris Gutzer	Child Care Home	Saskatchewan
Ida Haché	Family Child Care Provider	Québec
Sharon Hachey	ECCENB/SEPENB	New Brunswick
Mary Ann Haddad	Tache Community Day Care	Manitoba
Suzann Hanames	College of the North Atlantic	Newfoundland and Labrador
Shannon Harrison	Point Pleasant Child Care Centre	Nova Scotia
Norma Hatcher	International Friends Day Care Centre	Newfoundland and Labrador
John Hefler	Algonquin College	Ontario
France Henriques	Garderie Chez Tiago	New Brunswick